Lucas Wants to Become an Auto-Rickshaw Driver

Copyright © 2020 by A Devi Thangamaniam. All right reserved.

No part of this publication may be reproduced, distributed, or transmitted in any form or by any means, including photocopying, recording, or other electronic or mechanical methods, without the prior written permission of the author, except in the case of brief quotations embodied in critical reviews and certain other non-commercial uses permitted by copyright law.

Information: MiLu Children's Educational Source. www.my-willing.com

ISBN: 979-8-88525-437-3

Vroom Vroom

"I want to become an Auto-Rickshaw driver".

Lucas said.

Lucas lives in Denmark.
During his summer vacation,
he went to Sri Lanka.

He saw cars, buses, minivans, lorries, trucks, motorcycles,
scooters, bicycles, and auto-rickshaws.
When he saw the auto rickshaw, he was very excited to drive it.

Lucas has never seen Auto-Rickshaw before.

Auto-Rickshaw is a small vehicle.
People call **'Auto'** for short.

They call **'Three wheelers'** too,
because it has three wheels only.

People use Auto-Rickshaw for taxi.

Lucas and his sister Mia were so happy to
travel by Auto-Rickshaw.

They asked their parents for traveling again
and again by Auto.

They traveled many times by Auto
wherever they went outside.

Mom! **"I want to become an Auto-Rickshaw driver".**

Lucas said.

"Sure Lucas, Auto-Rickshaw driving is a wonderful job. Auto-Rickshaw drivers help people for traveling in many ways.

They drive place to place on people's request.

Reach the place on time.   Carrying their luggage.

Drive carefully with safely and security.

Work on day and night with shift basis.

Charging price is cheaper than other vehicles".

Mom said.

"Lucas! After you turn age eighteen you can become an **Auto-Rickshaw Driver.**

After you turn age eighteen, have to learn Auto-Rickshaw Driving Training. Then you can get Auto-Rickshaw Driving License". Mom said.

"Yes, Mom. After I turn age eighteen, I will learn Auto-Rickshaw Driving Training.

Then I will get Auto-Rickshaw Driving Licence and **I will be an Auto-Rickshaw Driver".** Lucas said.

Then Lucas and his sister Mia sang a song.

Vroom Vroom

Drive drive Auto drive

Will you drive?

Yes. I will drive

Drive best Auto drive

"Mom! I will drive Auto very carefully and follow the road's rules exactly. I will keep people safe and make them happy". Lucas said.

 "That's good Lucas. I appreciate about your caring. Safety is an important thing.

Everyone has to follow the road's rules exactly. Road rules guide to safe people's life, protect vehicle damage, save time and money". Mom said.

"Yes, Mom. Everyone must follow the road rules exactly". Lucas and Mia said.

Vroom Vroom
Follow follow road's rules follow
Will you follow?
Yes. We will follow
Follow must road's rules follow

"Lucas! You need to wear the seat belt". Mia said.

"Yes, Mia". Lucas said.

"Correct, Mia. I am so proud of your excellent advice.

Wearing the seatbelt is protected and minimized injuries to drivers and passengers.

Drivers and passengers must wear a seat belt when they travel by vehicle.

Young children need to wear the child car seat belts when they travel by vehicle". Mom said.

"Yes, mom. When I travel by vehicle I wear the seat belt". Lucas said.
"Me too". Mia said.

"When I drive I will wear the seat belt too". Lucas said.

Vroom vroom

Wear wear seat belt wear

Will you wear?

Yes. We will wear

Wear safety seat belt wear

"Mom! Do the dog needs to wear a seat belt when they travel by vehicle"?
　　　　　　　　　　Lucas asked.

"Yes. Lucas! The dog needs to wear a seat belt when they travel by vehicle.

The smaller dog needs to wear a seat belt with the carrier when they travel by vehicle.

The smaller pets need to keep in the 'Pet cage' when they travel by vehicle.

When animals travel need to keep comfortable, safe, and happy. Isn't it"?
　　　　　　　　　　Mom asked.

"Yes, Mom. Animals must be kept comfortable, safe, and happy when they travel". Lucas and Mia said.

"I appreciate you for caring about animals when traveling".
　　　　　　　　　　Mom said.

Vroom vroom

Care care pets care

Will you care?

Yes. we will care

Care comfort pets care

8

"Mom! I will stop my Auto in the traffic red light". Lucas said.

"Yes, Lucas. I am very glad of your paid attention, to obey the traffic red light.

The traffic signal lights are communicated to drivers and pedestrians.

It guides them to do their work, by taking turns and controlling the crisis.

Remember the yellow light is to notify slow down and prepare to stop.

Then the red light, notify bring your Auto to the complete stop". Mom said

"Yes, Mom. I will respect the traffic signal lights. Everyone must take a turn and do their work without crisis". Lucas said.

Vroom vroom

Stop stop red light appear stop

Will you stop?

Yes. I will stop

Stop appear red light stop

9

"Lucas! Whenever you see the traffic stop sign, always, it's important to bring your Auto to a complete stop too.  It appears at the intersections, schools, and houses zone.

The traffic stop sign helps drivers and pedestrians.

Always, when they stop, can decide who has the right-of-way, and then they will take turns and do their actions.

This method is helping to reduce the danger ahead". Mom said.

"Yes, Mom. Everyone must obey the traffic stop sign and helps to reduce the danger ahead".
Always I will obey when I see the traffic stop sign". Lucas said.
"Me too" Mia said.

"I am really happy about you, for obeying the traffic stop sign". Mom said

Vroom vroom

Stop stop always stop

Will you stop?

Yes. we will stop

Stop always, traffic stop sign stop

"Mom! I will manage the driving speed limit". Lucas said.

"Yes, Lucas. It is a great safety practice.
The speed limits are designed for the safety of drivers, passengers, bicyclists, and pedestrians.

The speed limit is balancing the higher, lower speeds and help in managing drive". Mom said.

"Yes, mom. The speed limit is very important. I will observe the speed limit and drive my Auto correctly". Lucas said.

"Yes, Lucas. I like your thoughtful way, of managing the driving speed limit". Mom said.

Vroom Vroom

Limit limit speed limit

Will you limit?

Yes. I will limit

Limit manage speed limit

"Mom! I need cell phone". Lucas said.

"That's correct Lucas. You need cell phone too.

When you drive, if people call, you park nearest parking place and answer the phone.

When you drive, talk, or type or read text messages over the cell phone, your eyes distract you from driving.
It will make a dangerous accident"
Mom said.

"Yes, Mom. When I drive I will turn off my cell phone. Always I will focus on driving". Lucas said.

Vroom Vroom

Away away Cell phone away

Will you away?

Yes. I will away

Away driving time Cell phone away

"Mom! I need headphone too". Lucas said.

"Lucas! Driving time listening to the radio, watching the video directly, or with headphones or wireless earbuds or earphones, can reduce driving attention.

The sound and pictures are easily distracted from driving attention. Finally, lead to the dangerous accident". Mom said.

"Yes, mom. When I drive I will avoid listening to the radio, watching the video directly, or with devices.

When I drive always, I will focus on the road sign only, and pay full attention for driving". Lucas said.

"Yes, Lucas. I am so happy for hearing from you, to avoid electronic devices while driving". Mom said.

Vroom Vroom

Remove remove devices remove

Will you remove?

Yes. I will remove

Remove when drive devices remove

13

"Lucas! You need to eat before driving" Mia said.

"Yes, I will Mia". Lucas said.

"This is good advice, Mia.
During the driving time eating, drinking and chewing gum will be distracted from driving".
Mom said.

"I agree Mom.
I will eat and drink before getting on the Auto.

During the driving time, I will avoid chewing gum too.

Always I will full concentration on driving". Lucas said.

"Lucas! I welcome you to your wonderful practice". Mom said.

Vroom Vroom

Avoid avoid food avoid

Will you avoid?

Yes. I will avoid

Avoid while driving food avoid

"Lucas! You need to cancel the sound while driving". Mia said.

"Sure, Mia". Lucas said.

"It's correct Mia, I appreciate your healthier advice.

Lucas! You always need to cancel the sound like music, horn, engine, tires, and brakes.

The sound leads to headaches, tension, stress, increases heart rate, changes in breathing, and more for drivers, passengers, and animals.

It can be very dangerous and may result in severe accidents too". Mom said.

"Yes, mom. I will completely cancel the sound when I drive. I will keep people's and animals' minds calm". Lucas said.

"This is a great habit, Lucas. People and animals need a relaxed, and peaceful environment. We need to help them". Mom said.

Vroom Vroom
Cancel cancel sound cancel
Will you cancel?
Yes. I will cancel
Cancel completely sound cancel

"Mom! I will keep the First Aid Kits in my auto". Lucas said.

"Yes, Lucas. This is very good knowledge about emergency care.

Sometimes anyone gets hurt, the First Aid Kits help until get emergency support". Mom said.

"Yes, Mom. I will keep the First Aid Kit in my auto. It can help to care and reduce the risks of the situation". Lucas said.

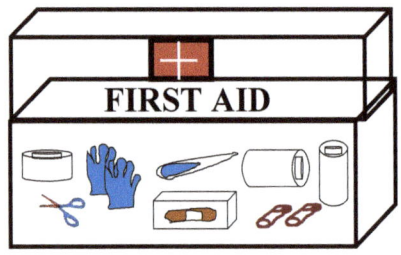

"I am so proud of your knowledge, of keeping First Aid Kits in your auto". Mom said.

Vroom Vroom

Keep keep First Aid Kits keep

Will you keep?

Yes. I will keep

Keep immediate aids keep

"Mom! I will need to wear High - Visibility Safety Cloth" Lucas said.

"Yes, Lucas. This is proper guidance for greater safety.

The wearing of high-visibility cloth is increasing a person's visibility.

It prevents accidents caused by traffic and a low-level lighting environment.

Lucas! Sometimes emergency situation happen, you and passengers need to get down from the auto on the way.

Wearing High-Visibility Safety Cloth shows up in higher light. Other drivers can notice from farther away". Mom said.

"Yes, Mom. I will keep High Visibility Safety Cloth in my auto and wear it in the emergency situation". Lucas said.

"Lucas! I am very delighted of your meaningful understanding". Mom said.

Vroom Vroom

wear wear safety cloth wear

Will you wear?

Yes. I will wear

Wear improve safety cloth wear

17

"Lucas! When you meet the passengers greet them". Mia said.

"Yes, I will Mia". Lucas said.

"Yes, Mia. This is another wonderful piece of advice.

Lucas! Every day you will meet different kinds of people. You will meet children, elders, patients, people with special needs, and more.

They have different needs. You always be positive, hospitable, and help to them". Mom said.

"Yes, mom. I will be polite, respectful, and help them". Lucas said.

"I am so happy of your treating way of people". Mom said.

Vroom Vroom

Respect respect equal respect

Will you respect?

Yes. I will respect

Respect always people respect

Lucas was so happy.

He was pretending to drive an Auto-Rickshaw.

Vroom, Vroom

"**I will be an Auto-Rickshaw Driver**. After age eighteen. I will be the best Auto-Rickshaw driver in the world". Lucas said.

Lucas!

"I will travel with you by your auto".

Mia said.

"Lucas! Me too".

Mom said.

Vroom, Vroom

Drive drive Auto drive

Will you drive?

Yes. I will drive

Drive best auto drive

Lucas will drive …..

"Welcome everyone, to travel with me by my auto. Have a happy, safe, and comfortable travel". Lucas said.

www.ingramcontent.com/pod-product-compliance
Lightning Source LLC
LaVergne TN
LVHW072133060526
838201LV00072B/5025